Original title:
A Sip of Paradise

Copyright © 2025 Creative Arts Management OÜ
All rights reserved.

Author: Oliver Bennett
ISBN HARDBACK: 978-1-80581-483-2
ISBN PAPERBACK: 978-1-80581-010-0
ISBN EBOOK: 978-1-80581-483-2

The Brightness of Each Quenching Drop

In a glass so cold and tall,
I see my dreams begin to sprawl.
Lemons dance, the icebergs grind,
A sip of joy, oh what a find!

Each bubble laughs, a playful sprite,
Tickling tongues in sheer delight.
Cherries wink from frosted shores,
While mint leaves plot, behind closed doors.

My drink's a clown, it wears a hat,
With jests and japes, it jokes like that.
Slurping sounds, oh what a spree,
This glass of giggles just for me!

So raise your cup to every drop,
Let's lock the door, and never stop.
With every sip, I'm on a quest,
To make a toast to liquid jest!

Ocean's Secrets Wrapped in Aromas

The sea's perfume drifts on the air,
A fruity mix beyond compare.
With pineapples in diving gear,
And coconuts spinning without fear.

Waves giggle as they splash the shore,
They tickle toes, and beg for more.
Salt and sugar, what a blend,
Together they make the perfect friend.

Seashells sing of cocktails bright,
While ocean crabs prepare for flight.
Cocktail umbrellas—tiny hats,
Are worn by silver-finned chitchats.

With every wave, a sloshy cheer,
Drink it up, there's nothing to fear!
These secrets shared, we'll toast and sway,
In this sea of laughter, let's stay!

Toast to Tranquility

Raise a glass, clink it high,
With juice that's brighter than the sky.
If it spills, no need to fret,
Just blame it on the pickled pet.

We'll sip and laugh 'til we fall,
Who knew this grape juice had a call?
Each ounce of bliss, a giggle shared,
Life's too short to be impaired.

Fragrant Fantasies

Lemonade scented like a dream,
It whispers sweetly, or so it seems.
A splash of mint, a dash of fun,
Bubbles pop—let's keg this one!

Watermelon giggles in the sun,
A fruit parade that's just begun.
Let's blender dance and sing out loud,
Watch the leafy peas get proud!

Mosaic of Flavors

Peachy chunks in a silly bowl,
Dance on spoons like they're on a stroll.
Strawberries laugh, they roll and play,
Just don't eat the ones from yesterday!

A swirl of joy in every sip,
Tasting mastery on a wobbly trip.
Let's blend the happy, twist the tart,
With every drop, we steal the heart!

Savoring Solitude

In my glass, I see a joke,
A little chaos, then I stroke.
Lemon twist and honey's hug,
Sippin' slow, just like a slug.

Alone brings giggles, what a scene,
With each sip, I feel so keen.
A little waltz around my chair,
Cheers to the fun that's always there!

Horizon's Melody in a Mug

In a cup, the sun gets stuck,
But hey, it's just my luck!
Sugar swirls like a dance,
Who needs a second chance?

I sip while planes swoosh by,
In dreams, I try to fly.
But all I find is foam,
And thoughts of going home.

The Colorful Nectar of Paradise

A drink that's bright like the sun,
Sipping this, I think I've won!
Flavors bounce like monkeys play,
Turning drab into a ballet.

Lime and berry sing a tune,
Underneath the probing moon.
It may stain my shirt just right,
But drinking's pure delight!

Lost in Sips of Ocean Wind

Waves dance in my ceramic friend,
Each sip is a journey, no end.
Sandy toes and giggles loud,
A drink that makes me feel proud!

I accidentally spill a bit,
But laughter's where I truly sit.
Tides may rise and fall away,
But my mood is here to stay!

Balmy Night and Sweet Infusions

Under stars, I clink my glass,
Wit and laughter come to pass.
Drinks so sweet, they dance on lips,
Waves of joy in little sips!

Fireflies join the evening fun,
Strangers turn to friends, we run!
Bubbles float like tales grown old,
In these nights, all hearts turn bold!

Tasting the Melody of the Breeze

A glass of laughter, chilled and bright,
Dancing flavors take to flight.
Whispers of fruit, a playful tease,
Each sip a giggle in the breeze.

Strawberry giggles, lemon cheers,
Frothy bubbles dance like peers.
With every swig, the sun will shine,
As we toast to life, in good time.

Pour another round, let worries cease,
Mirthful moments, a joyful feast.
On this merry pathway we tread,
With cups raised high, no room for dread.

Reflections in Sunset Sips

Golden sunsets in a glass,
Every swirl a swirling laugh.
We sip the hues, bright and cheeky,
Each taste a joke, oh so sneaky!

Twilight cocktails with silly names,
Mixing laughter in crazy games.
Banana split, a tipsy craze,
We swirl and twirl, lost in a daze.

As night falls softly, drinks in hand,
We toast to dreams, oh so grand.
Laughter echoes, a joyful din,
With every sip, the fun begins!

The Brew of Dreams and Distant Shores

In a teacup filled with sunny cheer,
Every drop whispers, 'No need to fear!'
Coconut waves and mango smiles,
We laugh and dream across the miles.

A pinch of salt, a splash of fun,
Tasting the laughter, never done.
With each warm sip, we chase the night,
Under stars that twinkle bright.

Sipping joy from distant shores,
Making memories, opening doors.
With every gaffe, a hearty cheer,
In this quirky brew, we have no fear!

Sunshine Steeped in Liquid Joy

Sunshine brewed with giggles tight,
Bubbly laughter, oh what a sight!
Lemon zest and honey cheer,
Every gulp brings you near.

Twirling straws, a silly race,
Tasting joy, we find our place.
In a whirl of colors and sounds,
We sip the fun, where laughter abounds.

In this cup of mirth, we discover,
Silliness wraps like a soft cover.
So let us pour and let us play,
With sunshine steeped, we'll seize the day!

Tropical Whispers

Upon the beach a coconut winks,
With shades of green, it surely thinks.
The parrot laughs, a silly sound,
As waves of laughter swirl around.

A piña colada does a dance,
While pineapples prance in a hula trance.
The sun is hot, the sand's a tease,
And seagulls steal your chips with ease.

Mangoes roll like playful balls,
As tourists stumble, heedless falls.
Flip-flops flying, sunburned backs,
The ice cream truck now takes no slack.

In tropical air, fun fills our days,
With fruit that smiles in delightful ways.
So raise your glass and cheers to cheer,
In paradise, we find good beer!

Celestial Brews

In a mug of stars, I brew my fun,
Mixing comets till the day is done.
A splash of laughter, a dash of glee,
Galactic sips, just for me!

The Milky Way, it twirls and spins,
While asteroids shake their cosmic fins.
I sip my drink while aliens tease,
Offering me intergalactic cheese.

Sipping coffee on a moonlit night,
With sugar comets putting up a fight,
It's bubbly joy in every sip,
Sweetened stardust gives a skip.

Celestial brews, a cheeky delight,
With every gulp, the world's so bright.
So raise your cup to the cosmic wonders,
And avoid those pesky thunderous blunders!

Nectar of the Sun

Bees buzz here, their honey flows,
As flowers giggle, striking poses.
Sunshine spills a golden drink,
The garden dances, don't you think?

A watermelon laughs, it's quite a sight,
As ants join in the fruit-filled fight.
Tomatoes blushing in sun's embrace,
Making salsa with a spicy grace.

Jugs of lemonade, oh what a treat,
With sprigs of mint, it can't be beat.
Lemon slices dance on rim so fine,
While kids play tag, sipping the brine.

Juicy fruits in a merriment spree,
With every sip, pure harmony.
So come and join this fruity affair,
In sunshine's nectar, there's joy to share!

Serene Sips

A hammock sways beneath the trees,
With lazy breezes, life's a breeze.
The pitcher's full, the ice clinks loud,
As sun-kissed folks drift like a cloud.

Lemonade dreams in a sleepy town,
Where even the ants don a crown.
A turtle's sipping chia seed tea,
While tea bags argue in a spree.

Sipping slow with smiles and grins,
The cheerful chatter never thins.
The sun dips low, a painted sky,
With cookies freshly baked nearby.

So grab a cup and take a dive,
In serene sips, we come alive.
With laughs and joy, we slowly flow,
In soft twilight's warm, friendly glow!

Lush Bliss in Every Gulp

In a coconut cup, I take my chance,
Sipping sunlight, I join the dance.
Kiwi wiggles, and mango spins,
Laughter bubbles, where joy begins.

Straw umbrellas wave in delight,
As the drink spills, what a sight!
A splash of color, a sprinkle of cheer,
I'm the king of the beach, with nothing to fear.

Slurping quickly, I make a mistake,
Straw gets stuck, oh what a quake!
Friends are chuckling, I'm in a twist,
Nature's a joker, I can't resist.

But in this chaos, I find my bliss,
Every sip feels like a sunny kiss.
In the world of flavor, I take the crown,
With my goofy drinks, I'll never drown.

Tropical Reverie in a Glass

Peachy dreams dance in the breeze,
Drinks like this put me at ease.
Mango mischief, a zesty swig,
Why is the glass doing a jig?

Pineapples cheer from the sidelines,
While I concoct these fruity designs.
With every gulp, I start to sway,
Who knew fruit could lead me astray?

Giggling lemons join the scene,
Their tangy remarks are quite obscene.
Coconut laughs as it drops in,
This tropical party's a wild spin.

I never thought about a fruit's charm,
Yet here I am causing alarm.
In a kingdom where flavors conspire,
I'm crowned the queen of this fruity choir.

A Dance with the Gentle Tides

Waves giggle, tickling my toes,
A minty potion, the laughter flows.
With every sip, the ocean winks,
And I'm dancing, who needs drinks?

Salt in the air, and foam on my chin,
With every wave, I tumble in.
A jellyfish pinches, oh what a game,
In this frothy fun, I'm never the same.

Sipping secrets from the sea,
What's the catch? Just you and me!
Fish are blushing, they swim away,
As I disco with my drink today.

The tide pulls back, I'm caught off guard,
Slipping and sliding, I'm the goofball bard.
But with every wave and tumble I take,
I find joy in chaos, for laughter's sake.

The Joys of Island Brews

A smoothie swirl, so thick and sweet,
My blender sings a tropical beat.
Banana boogie, berry twist,
In this flavor world, I can't resist.

Flavors mingling, like friends at play,
They cheer for more, don't fade away!
A splash of rum, a dash of fun,
As laughter bubbles, part of the run.

Sipping slow, I see the sun,
Behind my shades, oh this is fun!
KIWI high-fives and pomegranate cheers,
I'm the MVP, toasting with peers.

So let's raise our glasses, make a toast,
To island brews and moments we boast.
In this fruity chaos, so bright and bold,
We laugh together, growing old.

Elysian Tastes

In a glass I see a potion,
Sparkling bubbles cause commotion.
Sipping slow, oh what a tease,
Grape juice spilled, oh quel surprise!

Straws and umbrellas, quite the sight,
Floating pineapples, what a delight!
Lemons dancing in the foam,
Who knew snacks could feel like home?

A cherry plops in with a splash,
My drink is now a fruity mash!
Bananas giggle, peaches grin,
I laugh out loud, let the fun begin!

With every sip, a burst of cheer,
Strawberry laughter fills the near.
In a cup, the joy expands,
Elysian tastes in funky hands!

Bliss in a Bloom

Petals swirl in a cocktail glass,
Mixing flavors oh so brash.
Daisies shout, 'We're in the mix!'
Tulips giggle, pulling tricks.

Margarita smiles with her lime,
Dance of flavors, oh so prime!
Sipping joyyard, flowers sway,
Turning every bump to play!

Honey bees buzz for more delight,
While daisies dig in for a bite.
Cactus winks with a cheeky grin,
With every sip, we all win!

Petal power in every drop,
Laughter up, and worries flop.
In this bloom, we find our bliss,
A glass of fun, who could resist?

Essence of Euphoria

Coconut shavings in a shake,
Banana peels make no mistake.
Lime wheels roll with wild intent,
This drink's a party, heaven-sent!

Twirling paper straws in pink,
They frolic 'round, they leap and wink.
Orange slices wear tiny hats,
As fizzy bubbles dance like cats.

A sip of giggles, flavors twine,
Pineapple dreams, a fun design!
Grapefruit jests, 'Come have a sip!'
With every chuckle, I take a trip!

In this cup, I find pure bliss,
A burst of joy, I cannot miss.
With fruity laughter, smiles in tow,
Essence of euphoria, let it flow!

Reflections in a Glass

In a tumbler a storm brews,
Cucumber slices, oh how they choose!
Mint leaves dance, a julep's waltz,
Lime so cool, it's never false.

Twirling shadows cast on ice,
Laughter echoes, tasting nice.
Peachy nectar, sweet and bold,
A potion's tale yet to be told.

Bubbles hum a merry tune,
As I drink beneath the moon.
Each sip's a riddle, lemony fiddle,
This glass of giggles, oh what a middle!

Reflections ripple, time stands still,
Each thought a tickle, such a thrill.
With every swallow, joy amassed,
In this little world, I'll raise my glass!

Enchanted Waters

In a cup with magic, I take my chance,
A splash of joy leads to a silly dance.
There's pineapple and laughter, a wobbly twist,
Take a sip, my friend! You can't resist!

With every gulp, the giggles grow,
The ocean's whispers become a show.
Sipping sunshine, it gives me glee,
Why save the good stuff for a fancy tea?

Swirling colors, a rainbow sways,
Each drink a jester in whimsical ways.
The mango winks, the coconut grins,
Pour some fun where the laughter begins.

So cheers to the bubbles, the froth and cheer,
Let's toast to the silly, the drinks we hold dear.
For in every sip, there's a joke to find,
A splash of mischief, naturally kind.

Soothing Serenade

In a glass of dreams, I find my chill,
Strawberries sing, as I sip my fill.
The ice cubes dance, a tango so sweet,
Fruity melodies make my heart skip a beat.

Each sip's a chuckle, a playful jest,
Grapefruit giggles put taste to the test.
Lime with a wink and mint with a spin,
This cocktail's humor makes every grin.

Raspberry blush, oh it teases the tongue,
Telling me tales of when we were young.
As bubbles burst like balloons in air,
I laugh out loud without a care.

So here's to the drinks that tickle the soul,
Each flavor savored makes the body whole.
Raise your glass high, let the laughter ensue,
With every comforting sip, I toast to you!

Harvest of Happiness

Gather 'round, folks, for a whimsical brew,
Apple cider wishes with a hint of glue!
It sticks in your heart, makes your belly shake,
With every sweet sip, it's a funny mistake.

Caramel fizzes dance on the tongue,
There's joy in the chaos when you're feeling young.
Sipping sweet nectar, it's laughter we sow,
Giggles and snickers—come join the show!

Plump berries bouncing like kids on the floor,
Their fervent delights really do ask for more.
Mixing and shaking, oh what a quest,
Each drink's an adventure—come join the fest!

So raise up a toast to this vibrant blend,
To hops, jokes, and laughter that never end.
In every bright flavor, let happiness grow,
A harvest of smiles in every flow.

Island Infusions

On a dreamy isle, where coconuts sway,
I mix a concoction bright as the day.
The parrot cackles, oh what a sight,
As I sip and giggle, tasting pure delight.

Guava whispers secrets with every sip,
The sand tickles toes, oh what a trip!
With pineapple hats and banana ties,
The fruit parade makes the best surprise.

Mango and laughter bloom side by side,
In every glass, a playful ride.
The sunbeams twinkle, inviting a grin,
Where the fun begins, let the chaos spin!

So here's to the beach, to the waves and cheer,
With each silly sipper, we banish the drear.
Let's raise our cups to the fruity escapade,
In this island haven, let fun never fade!

Oasis in a Cup

In a mug so round and bright,
A tropical drink, pure delight.
With a twist of lime, it laughs and sighs,
Every gulp brings coconut skies.

Straws like flamingos, oh so chic,
Sipping joy, we feel unique.
With every slurp, our worries scoff,
This little oasis, we just can't scoff.

Cheers to the ice that starts to melt,
In this warm brew, our hearts are felt.
We toast to laughter, friendship's blend,
In this cup, let the fun not end!

Blissful Brews

A steaming cup of something grand,
Spilling sweetness, oh so bland.
With bubbles dancing, a fruity twist,
One tiny sip, can't resist!

We giggle as we make a toast,
To sips of joy we love the most.
Mango overflows like a silly dream,
In this brew, we float and beam.

With every sip, our worries fade,
This funny drink, our sweet parade.
So raise your cup, give cheers anew,
To blissful brews, the fun we brew!

Essence of Eden

A colorful cup of fruity cheer,
With each sip, the world feels clear.
Papaya giggles, kiwi grins,
In this elixir, mischief begins!

Lemon drops and tangerine,
Spilling giggles, oh what a scene!
With every gulp, we swirl and spin,
A wild drink where laughs begin.

The ice chimes in like a grand parade,
Pouring laughter, our finest braid.
In this nectar, we find our zest,
A shiny pot where joy is best!

Lush Liquid Journeys

From glass to lips, a travel spree,
Bright flavors swirl, come dance with me!
A splash of chaos, a drip of fun,
In every taste, the laughter's spun.

A kaleidoscope of tastes awaits,
With every sip, our joy elates.
Beneath the sun, the giggles flow,
As we sip on this funny show.

So toast to drinks that make us smile,
With each sip, let's linger awhile.
For in this cup, we're free and bold,
Lush journeys waiting, treasures untold!

Dreams Brewed Beneath Palm Trees

In the shade where coconuts sway,
I spilled my drink in a silly way.
Laughter echoes through the night,
As we toast to the moon's soft light.

With a wink and a twist of fate,
My friends join in, oh isn't it great?
We mix our dreams under starry beams,
And giggle at wild, whimsical schemes.

A parrot squawks, "Is that your drink?"
I chuckle, "No, it's just the pink!"
Sand between toes, the breeze in our hair,
Who knew paradise starts with a dare?

Let the waves of laughter roll by,
As we sip from coconut, oh my!
A toast to night's silly, bright tease,
Where dreams get brewed beneath palm trees.

Oasis in a Teacup

In a cup of tea, I found my bliss,
But then it spilled, oh what a miss!
Sugar ants marched in a long line,
Claiming my drink, oh that's just fine!

With a dash of lime and a hint of glee,
I added a splash—what chaos to see!
Friends with giggles, we stir the pot,
An oasis made of laughter, why not?

A teapot sings as it starts to whistle,
"Fill me up or just let me drizzle!"
So we dance in the kitchen, a silly waltz,
Who knew tea parties had such faults?

In this mug, flavors collide,
With every sip, our laughter won't hide.
An oasis brightened by joy and cheer,
Let's swirl in a teacup, without fear!

The Elixir of Tranquil Waters

In the stream, I dipped my toes,
But slipped right in, oh how it goes!
Splashing water everywhere,
Our laughter mingles with the air.

With a leaf as a cup, I took a sip,
A frog jumped in, a boating trip!
We paddled together, how absurd,
A chorus of croaks, not a single word.

Waves of giggles flow like the tide,
With each little splash, our worries slide.
Nature's drink brings joy anew,
While a turtle joins our weirdest crew.

So here's to moments, silly and bright,
Where waters dance in the warm moonlight.
An elixir of joy, laughter, and cheer,
Let's dive in together, there's nothing to fear!

Breeze-Kissed Bliss

Oh what a day with the wind at play,
I winked at a cloud, it rolled away!
My drink in hand, I twirl and spin,
Chasing sunshine while birds rush in.

The breeze has tricks, it flips my hat,
I chase it down, how absurd is that?
Laughter trails as I stumble and run,
Who knew wild fun could weigh so much fun?

A gust whispers secrets, tickles my ears,
I toast to the clouds, shedding no tears.
With each breeze-kissed step, we jiggle and sway,
Creating joy in the sun's warm ray.

So raise your glass, let's dance till night,
With laughter echoing, oh what a sight!
Breeze-kissed moments, so pure, so free,
In this whimsical world, come sip with me!

A Taste of Coastal Euphoria

Sandy toes and salty air,
Lemonade spills without a care,
Seagulls laugh and steal my fries,
While I sip beneath blue skies.

Waves that crash with goofy grace,
Sunburned nose, a silly face,
The ice cream melts, a sticky treat,
As I dance on sun-soaked street.

Beach ball bounces, laughter flies,
Chasing friends, with silly cries,
A sip of joy, so brightly gleamed,
In every wave, I feel redeemed.

Sipping nectar of the fun,
Underneath the blazing sun,
Life's a brew of happy sighs,
In this coastal paradise, laughs rise.

Sunset Elixirs and Moonlight Brews

As the sun dips down to play,
I mix my drinks in a bubbly way,
Pineapple dreams and coconut whirls,
Under stars, my laughter twirls.

Shaken not stirred, with a twist of lime,
Each sip feels like a joke in rhyme,
The moon winks at my clumsy dance,
In cocktail chaos, I find romance.

Jelly shots and silly cheers,
The night is young, dissolve my fears,
With every gulp, we share a song,
In bubbles of joy, where all belong.

Floating whims and swirling glee,
Together sipping, just you and me,
As twilight seals this merry brew,
We toast to fun, the whole night through.

Sunkissed Bliss in Every Drop

Morning brews with sleepy sighs,
Coffee dances, oh what a rise,
With whipped cream clouds and sprinkles bright,
Each sip's a cheer, oh what a sight!

Lemonade laughter, fizzy and bold,
Sweet summer stories that never grow old,
I tip my glass to the bees that hum,
As I concoct more sips of fun.

Sparkling waters with playful zest,
Hydration's never been this blessed,
Friends guffaw with cups in hand,
While we bask in the golden sand.

With each refreshing, joyful cheer,
Sunkissed happiness, we hold dear,
Life's a party with every gulp,
Sippin' bliss, we happily sulk.

Bottled Memories of Summer

Caught in a jar, sunshine's glow,
I pop the cap and let it flow,
Strawberry wishes, peachy dreams,
In every sip, the laughter gleams.

Picnic time with fizzy pops,
Watermelon chunks and giggle drops,
A stumble here, a spill right there,
Memories lost in the sunlit air.

Chugging joy like it's a race,
I wear the drink with a silly face,
From grape to mango, flavors collide,
Summer tastes with friends by my side.

In bottles filled with laughter sweet,
We toast to moments, oh so neat,
With sips of joy, our hearts will hum,
Bottled bliss, where fun is from.

Call of the Coral Breeze

In the land where jellyfish tango,
And sea cucumbers wear bright hats,
I sip on water from a coconut,
And try not to trip on fat brats.

The parrot named Polly chuckles loud,
As I dance with a crab in the sun,
His claws on my toes, oh, such a crowd!
Yet laughter's the fruit of good fun.

The fish in the sea do a jig,
While I'm stuck in my flip-flop fate,
A toast to the ones who just dig,
Their tails in the sand and elate.

Underneath the palm trees so green,
With a smoothie that's bright like a glow,
Life's just a beachy routine,
And I'm caught in its whimsical flow.

Botanical Serenade by the Sea

With sunflowers swaying, I sing,
To the breeze that tickles my face,
A watermelon slice is my bling,
Though I might drop it; what a disgrace!

The lilacs conspire in a plot,
As seagulls dive-bomb for my snack,
I yell, "Hey, you can't have that! Not!
Just back off, or I'll throw you a whack!"

Lemonade rivers run down my chin,
As I trip over basil's tall stalks,
The garden erupts in a spin,
With vegetables mocking my walks.

In my floral hat, I parade,
To a tune played by crickets with zest,
Each fluttering leaf serenades,
A laugh in this garden fest.

Elixirs Crafted by Nature

In glasses of fruit, I concoct,
A blend that could bubble and roar,
But with every sip, I'm shocked,
I find vinegar, not a sweet score!

The mixers may tease and perplex,
As I shake up a cocktail of glee,
Pepper and mint? What's coming next?
A dragonfruit laugh—oh, that's me!

Citrus fruits roll off my hands,
Like the jester in a grand show,
I'm chaos in nature's demands,
Yet laughing like it's all in the flow.

In this banquet of colors and flavor,
I dive into salads with cheer,
Nature's the chef; I'm the waver,
Mixing up joy and good beer.

The Symphony of Fragrant Waters

Beneath the sea, a laugh does swell,
As octopuses beat on the drums,
The bubbles arise; what tales they tell,
Of fish that dance and wiggle their rums!

Flowery waves, so bright and bold,
They tease with scents like springtime cakes,
But watch for seaweed's greenish hold,
It's a trap for the careless mistakes!

I dip my toes in lemon-lime foam,
While dolphins join, wearing sunglasses,
Each splash sends my worries back home,
And I giggle at oceanic passes.

The tide rolls in, takes the stage,
With laughter ringing across the bay,
In this concert of joy, I engage,
Just a splash in a colorful play.

A Pool of Beverage Bliss

In a world of fizzy dreams,
Float on cola streams.
Soda splash, a bubbly dance,
Who knew it could be such a chance?

Lemonade waterfalls will flow,
With sprinkles on top, in a rainbow show.
Ice cubes jive in happy loops,
While gummy bears join the fruity troops!

Pool noodles made of licorice sweet,
Dive right in, isn't this neat?
Cannonballs of fruit punch ring,
On beach towels, oh let's swing!

But wait! Oh no, don't spill!'
You'll find yourself in a fruity thrill.
Laughter bubbles as we all cheer,
In our drinks, summer's finally here!

Meeting the Shore of Sweet Waters

Oh, the beach is where we meet,
With cups of mango, oh so sweet.
The salt in the air, the drinks in our hands,
Making waves and grand plans!

Pineapple umbrellas shade our smiles,
As we sip and lounge for endless miles.
Watermelon boats bob in the sun,
A fruity fiesta, oh so fun!

Seagulls squawk, demanding a taste,
While we sip slowly, no rush, no haste.
Drinking dreams from coconut shells,
In this seaside haven, oh how it dwells!

With each gulp we giggle and cheer,
"In this paradise, we have nothing to fear!"
So here's to our cups, raise them high!
In this sweet water wonder, let's fly!

Dance of Flavors Under the Stars

Under a sky of bursting light,
Flavors twirl and shimmer bright.
A potion mix of raspberry thrill,
With a dash of mint to chill!

We swirl and sip, oh what a treat,
As fizzy drinks dance to the beat.
Every sip, a funky groove,
In our cups, the flavors move!

Lime and ginger tango with glee,
A zesty party, come join me!
Strawberries waltz with lemon zest,
In our fruity boogie, we're truly blessed!

The night is young, the laughter loud,
With fizzy cocktails, we feel proud.
So raise your glass to keep the night,
In this flavor dance, we are alright!

Garden of Fresh Brews and Wonders

In a garden where flavors bloom,
Lemon grass and mint perfume.
Tea leaves waltz in gentle breeze,
Come explore this drink delight, if you please!

Jugs of berry blends galore,
Lively potions, who could want more?
Strawberry rhubarb's in the mix,
With sparkling sips that do the tricks!

The flowers giggle as we sip,
Dance around with every dip.
Citrus trees swing and sway,
In this fresh brew garden, we play!

With each cup poured, a new surprise,
In this garden of wonder, our laughter flies.
So grab your flavors, don't be shy,
In this joyful brew, we'll laugh and sigh!

Elixir of Dreams

In a glass, a potion swirls,
Tasting sunshine, doing twirls.
Lemon peel and giggles blend,
Why does my chatty drink offend?

Bubbles dance like froggy feet,
Sipping slow, it's quite the feat.
One sip in, the hat's gone askew,
Dancing with my pet kangaroo!

Strawberry whispers, juicy jokes,
This elixir revives the folks.
Why is the straw always frayed?
It just craved a carnival parade!

With every sip, I feel the cheer,
Seeing pink elephants appear!
I toast to friends and wild delight,
A giggle fest, oh what a sight!

Garden of Delights

In a garden where lemons bloom,
I found a mix that cleared the gloom.
A twist of mint and laughter bright,
Makes sipping feel like pure delight!

Cucumbers swim, oh what a sight,
They dance around in pure sunlight.
Tiny ants join in the parade,
Did they think it was a charade?

Watermelons dressed like kings,
Quenching thirst while laughter sings.
With a splash, I spill, what a mess!
Guess my drink loves to impress!

Cocktails whisper sweet and sly,
As I sip, the clouds float by.
Each gulp a giggle, each laugh a cheer,
In this garden, all is clear!

Sun-Kissed Elixirs

Sunbeams dance on fizzy cheer,
Each sip brings smiles, no need for fear.
Pineapple giggles, oh so bright,
Guess I'll be a fruit delight tonight!

Tropical swirls in a crazy cup,
Mango winks, and I can't shut up.
Parrots squawking, joining in,
Why not let the fun begin?

Sipping breezes on my tongue,
My dance partner? A rubber duck lung!
He quacks an ode to summer nights,
As we twirl under starry sights.

In this elixir, joy's embraced,
Each sip is fiercely interlaced.
With laughter and the sun's own kiss,
I toast to life, it's pure bliss!

Liquid Daydreams

In shades of blue, my drink appears,
A splash of fun, and all my fears.
Grapes do cartwheels, cheers of glee,
Why is my drink now chasing me?

Waves of tart with a touch of sweet,
It's a carnival, what a treat!
Fruit-flavored clouds drift all around,
My giggles float without a sound.

Marshmallow fluff on top so grand,
Frothy fun made by my own hand.
Why does my drink sing off-key?
It's just trying to be free like me!

Liquid dreams in every glass,
Sip a bit, watch time just pass.
With silly straws that twist and loop,
I dive in joy, I join the soup!

Fragrant Waves of Joy

The ocean's perfume wafts near,
As seagulls squawk and spread good cheer.
With jellyfish doing waltz on sand,
I wonder if they're part of the band.

Sunblock on noses, what a sight,
One's a lobster tonight, oh what a fright!
Umbrellas tumble, chasing a breeze,
While kids toss sand, pretending to sneeze.

In flippers and floats, they swim with glee,
But one little fish is napping on me.
Sandy snacks in a conch shell dish,
Oops! There goes my jello, what a squishy wish!

We dance with crabs, their moves so slick,
While sunburned tourists strike a pose quick.
The tide rolls back, the beach is aglow,
And laughter echoes far as we go.

Savoring Sunlit Delights

Ice cream melting quicker than light,
It drips and splats, oh what a sight.
A bite of mango, it slips and swirls,
Sticky fingers and a giggle unfurls.

Sandwiches fly in a gusty breeze,
Mustard on toes, oh what a tease!
Lemonade splashes, a refreshing dart,
I drank it all! Now my belly's a tart.

Tanned toes wiggle in feathered flip-flops,
Chasing seagulls, laughing, no stops.
Saltwater tickles, a splash, a fling,
As I dance in the waves, oh what joy it brings!

With every bite, there's a chuckle near,
From pizzas that dance, to soda that cheers.
In this sunlit feast, a banquet so bright,
I say, what a day! Let's celebrate the light!

Driftwood Dreams and Lush Reveries

Driftwood castles in the sand abound,
Made by children, so crafty and sound.
But watch your step, there's a crab on guard,
Snapping his claws like a cute little bard.

Under palm fronds, I recline and muse,
Breezy whispers and gossiping shoes.
Mermaids giggle, tales twisted and bent,
As I try to sleep, but the sun never went.

With a splash and a laughter, hope floats by,
A fishy face pops up! Oh my, oh my!
Cannonballs echo, a watery cheer,
Every jump feels like a leap into cheer!

Dreams of coconuts swirl in the breeze,
Tropical moments that aim to please.
With driftwood dreams carried far and wide,
Life's a beach party, let the fun be our guide!

Essence of a Hidden Cove

In a cove where shadows dance and sway,
Sunburned tummies and laughter at play.
A treasure chest filled with chips and dip,
Watch out for seagulls on an all-out trip!

Pineapple hats on heads so round,
A fruity parade on the sandy ground.
The waves wobble and giggle with us,
As we all jump over waves, what a fuss!

Footprints decorate our sandy domain,
While sneaky crabs do their little dance again.
Tickling the toes, an aquatic tease,
In this hidden paradise, we do as we please.

With mermaid laughter and giggles galore,
We create our summer, we always want more.
As the sun dips low, we wave goodbye,
And sneak a sip of moonlight in the sky.

Cascade of Liquid Sunshine

The juice flew high, like a startled bird,
With splashes and giggles, it simply stirred.
I wore a crown of sticky sweet,
While laughter echoed, what a treat!

With citrus slices joining the fun,
The blender whirred, a wild run.
Lemon wedged with zesty flair,
Ends up dancing, floating in air!

A sip, a slurp, oh what a game,
My fruit salad's got all the fame.
But watch out, my friend, it's quite a toss,
That kiwi slid, oh what a loss!

As droplets shimmer, golden and bright,
My cup's a rainbow, a charming sight.
Every taste is a giggle parade,
In this fruity chaos, I'm never afraid!

Aroma of Adventurous Shores

On the beach, a cup, quite a charmer,
With coconut dreams wrapped round like armor.
Straws like flamingos, standing tall,
While seagulls squawk - oh, what a brawl!

With every sip, the ocean calls,
But watch your back, that wave enthralls!
Caught off guard, my drink took flight,
A splash of pineapple, what a sight!

Salted breezes bring stories to tell,
Of mango pirates on a fruit-fueled swell.
Lime so zesty, it tickles my nose,
While coconut curls help ward off woes!

But suddenly, my cup tips over,
And now it's a party – I spill like clover!
The tide brings laughter, we dance on the shore,
With fruity splashes, who could ask for more?

Tranquility Served Cold

In the fridge, a treasure awaits,
A chilled elixir that simply resonates.
Pour over ice with a wink of zest,
It's a mocktail party, come be my guest!

But watch the ice, oh, don't let it float!
It may come alive and start to gloat.
With sprigs of mint that smell like a dream,
We laugh as we plan our next wacky scheme.

A hint of ginger danced in the glass,
While my buddy named Tim thought he'd add some class.

But all he did was a blender collision,
Out came a smoothie with no clear vision!

Now it's fizzy, a dance on the lip,
With giggles and bubbles, we take a trip.
To slumber-land where drinks wear a crown,
In this chilled wonderland, we'll never frown!

Harvesting Hues of the Sun

Today we gather what the garden gives,
Tomatoes, peppers – oh, how it lives!
But one little berry had a wink in its eyes,
As it rolled off the table – such crafty surprise!

With laughter we dash, a fruit-fetching feat,
While Grandma shouts, "Don't let them eat!"
Strawberry jam in a glorious war,
Making everything stick – oh, what a score!

But when we pressed juice, oh what a scene,
The colors exploded, like a work of sheen.
From purple to red, my hands become art,
And soon we're all wearing our fruity heart!

As we clink our glasses, full of delight,
It's a rainbow reflection, glowing so bright.
With gnarled fingers and sticky charms,
In this sunny picnic, we warm in loves' arms!

Liquid Gold Under Starlight

In a glass filled with shimmer, oh what a sight!
Lemonade dancing, under the moonlight.
A straw made of candy, sweet and so bold,
   Sip slow, my friend, it's liquid gold.

Stars whisper secrets, the night is alive,
With every small sip, our giggles survive.
Tropical flavors, so zesty and bright,
Who knew a drink could feel so light?

Bubbles in chaos, fizz popping around,
Splashing the table, oh what a sound!
We toast to the madness, our drink's our delight,
Let's empty this pitcher, oh what a sight!

With laughter and cheers, and a clink of our cups,
We conjure the magic and drink till we're up.
So here's to the moments, both silly and bold,
   Raise high your glass, it's liquid gold!

Celestial Tastes of the Coast

Pineapple piña coladas, oh what a treat,
Surrounded by friends, on a warm sunny seat.
Sand between toes and drinks with a twist,
A flavor explosion, you won't want to miss!

Seagulls are squawking, they sense the affair,
While we sip our cocktails, without a care.
Meringue in the air, and laughter so loud,
Cheers to the day, we are quite the crowd!

Ocean waves crash as we drink with glee,
Make sure to keep those drinks spill-free!
In tropical bliss, we make merry boasts,
About our incredible, celestial toasts!

Funny hats on, and sunglasses so chic,
Each sip feels like summer, that's our mystique.
In this lively shindig, we dance with the flow,
Celestial sips, where our spirits glow!

Chasing the Horizon's Embrace

We chase our drinks like they're racing the sun,
Each one a delight, oh, what silly fun!
Margaritas with laughter, they swirl in a dance,
As we jest about life, we take every chance.

Gazing toward sunsets with straws in our hands,
Mixing odd flavors, oh, isn't life grand?
A splash of confusion, a twist of lime cheer,
Who knew sipping drinks could bring us such sheer?

Fruity concoctions that start exploding,
With every new flavor, our fun is unloading.
We paint our horizon with laughter so wide,
In this sippin' adventure, let's take a ride!

With each wave of laughter, we sip and we toast,
Creating a party, our very own boast.
Cheers to the silly, the laughter, the grace,
As we chase all the joy's sweet embrace!

Swaying Palms and Gentle Hues

Swinging in hammocks, drinks swaying with ease,
Coconut breezes, oh, what a tease!
Tropical shades, we sip and we sway,
Pretend we're on vacation, all night and day.

Mango madness and banana delight,
With silly little umbrellas, our drinks take flight.
Salt on our cheeks and the sun on our nose,
What's better than laughter? A sweet drink that glows!

We'd spill all our secrets in these charming cups,
As waves call our names, we're ready to sup.
With swaying palms dancing and joy on our faces,
Every sip brings more fun to our favorite places!

Under stars that twinkle, as we drink and we cheer,
Embracing the night, let's bring on the cheer!
With gentle hues brightening our goofy ways,
Let's savor each moment, till we greet new days!

Blossoms Floating in Brew

In a cup so round and wide,
Petals float like they just tried,
To swim the depths of tea so sweet,
But then they sneeze and lose their seat.

Lemon slices do a dance,
Twist and twirl, they take a chance,
But a nibble from the spoon,
Turns their jig into a tune.

Honey drips with silly glee,
Says, "Just add me, you'll see!"
But before it mingles with a frown,
It finds itself stuck on the brown.

Oh what fun in this mad brew,
A playdate for the flavors too,
With giggles bubbling, zest in each sip,
Who knew a drink could take such a trip!

Embrace of Citrus Dusk

As the sun dips low and glows,
Oranges start their nightly shows,
Wearing hats made of zest and skin,
They shout, "Join us, let's begin!"

Limes roll in with a cheeky grin,
Causing chaos, they spin and spin,
"Oh, come on, don't be so sour,
Join the party, it's our hour!"

Grapefruit jumped with agile flair,
Landed right in the drink with care,
But slipped and slid, quite the scene,
Said, "Who knew I could be so green?"

Bubbles rise like laughter shared,
Each sip comes with tales declared,
In a glass, a zestful fuss,
What's next? A tango on the bus!

Brewed Whispers of Wonder

In a pot, the leaves conspire,
Whispers of warmth, they never tire,
"Steep us longer for more cheer,"
"But we might spill—it's getting clear!"

The kettle sings a silly song,
"Add some cream, it won't be long!"
Yet splashes dance and join the spree,
Creating messes, oh so free!

Sugar cubes leap, they take a dive,
To make this brew come alive,
Each clink and clank adds comic flair,
As all the spices join the fair.

Laughing steam escapes the lid,
Brewing mischief, just like a kid,
A playful cup of pure delight,
Who knew sipping could be so bright?

Crystalline Coasts of Contentment

On the shore, the ice cubes crash,
With splashes loud, they make a splash,
They wobble, tumble, seem so bold,
Screaming, "Chill, we're ice, not gold!"

Mint leaves cheer like tiny flags,
Waving dreams in little jags,
"Let's freeze the sun, let's frolic free,
In this drink, let's just be!"

A cherry floats, oh what a sight,
It holds a party, pure delight,
Raspberry swirls join in the fun,
And say, "We're here, let's not just run!"

The horizon glimmers, drinks unite,
As laughter in the glass takes flight,
Sipping joy, oh what a draw,
Who knew contentment could be so raw?

Dreamy Draughts

In a glass, the sun has caught,
A sip of bliss, oh what a thought!
With ice cubes dancing, wearing hats,
How silly of them, oh where they sat!

Lemon slices swim with glee,
Making jokes about the sea,
Mint leaves chuckle, fresh and bright,
Laughing softly in the light!

Fruity laughter fills the air,
With every gulp, we shed our care,
A fizzy bubble makes a run,
Across our lips, it's so much fun!

So raise your glass, let's celebrate,
This potion's giggle won't be late,
For in this cup, adventures flow,
A funny twist, oh don't you know?

Journeys of the Palate

A fruity road trip, what a ride,
Grapes driving fast, with kiwi as guide,
Banana is the rear-view champ,
Checking for flavors from the fruity camp!

Peaches surf on waves of cream,
While cherries giggle, living the dream,
Oranges brag about their zest,
Sipping juice as they're the best!

The bottle rolls down the hill,
With every drop, we laugh and thrill,
Tasting tales of summer's grace,
In this wild, fruity, joyous race!

So raise your goblet, toast the crew,
To hilarious flavors, tried and true,
In this journey, we'll not decline,
For every sip brings a funny line!

Whispers of Tropical Serenity

Coconuts whisper in the breeze,
As pineapples dance with cheeky tease,
Hibiscus laughs with a twist of lime,
Charming us all, keeping perfect time!

Mangoes flirt with the setting sun,
While passionfruit's joke is second-to-none,
A teasing wave, a laughing tide,
As they frolic, side by side!

Laughter bubbles in coconut shells,
In this paradise, where joy dwells,
Grab a straw, take a funny drink,
Together we sip, together we think!

So here's to laughs, in every drop,
To flavors that dance and never stop,
In this drink, we'll laugh and play,
In whispers sweet, we hope to stay!

Nectar from the Sunlit Shore

A chilled concoction greets the day,
With giggles dancing in a fruity way,
Raspberries wink from their berry boats,
While while coconut frolics and promotes!

Strawberry clouds float in our cups,
Sipping sunshine, we cheer and sup,
Pineapple pirates find their treasure,
In every sip, unmeasurable pleasure!

So come and join this merry crew,
As watermelon wears a sailor's shoe,
With each taste, we break into song,
Laughing together, where we belong!

So raise a glass to the fun we find,
In nature's goods, sweetly intertwined,
Nectar flows where jokes abound,
In every bubbly drop, fun is found!

Sweet Symphonies of the Sea

The ocean sings a funny tune,
With dolphins dancing, making a swoon.
Seagulls squawk, as if in cheer,
While crabs join in, oh dear, oh dear!

A whale pops up, with a splash and a grin,
Flipping and flopping, it's a wild din.
Fish wear hats, just for the tease,
Fin-tastic fun on the salty breeze!

Shells clink together like glasses of wine,
Each wave brings laughter, it's so divine.
Starfish gossip on the sandy floor,
Secrets shared that we can't ignore!

So grab a boat, let's set them free,
To this blithe symphony near the sea.
With giggles and bubbles, come take a ride,
Life's a beach, let's enjoy the tide!

Showers of Sunset Serenades

The sun dips low, with a wink and a smile,
Colors dance wild, let's stay awhile.
Clouds play tag in a fiery glow,
While birds audition for the evening show.

A squirrel in shades, sipping on tea,
Claims it's the best view, just wait and see!
While daisies sway to the sunset song,
They giggle softly, 'Is this right or wrong?'

Fireflies buzz like an evening choir,
Their glow lights up our hearts with desire.
The moon joins in, wearing a hat,
Whispering secrets to the night, how about that?

So let's toast to hues, both silly and bright,
With laughter and love, our spirits take flight.
In this splendor, let's dance and twirl,
Under the magic where joys unfurl!

Brews from the Bounty of Earth

In the kitchen, pots start to sing,
While carrots prance, adding their zing.
Tomatoes blush, feeling so bold,
Spicing up tales that were never told.

A cup of mud? Oh, what a tease!
With ants as baristas, serving up these.
"More sugar, please!" the mushrooms cry,
As broccoli laughs and gives a sly sigh.

Nature's nectar in jars all around,
Each sip a riddle, in taste we're bound.
Garlic winks, saying, "Don't be shy,"
While peppers strut in a flavorsome tie.

So raise your glass, let's savor the fun,
In this crazy kitchen, meals weigh a ton.
With every sip, let giggles proceed,
Brews from the earth bring joy we all need!

Echoes of Laughter in Every Drink

In every glass, a giggle awaits,
Bubbly bubbles cheer, 'Open the gates!'
The soda can dances on kitchen floors,
While juice boxes belt out a chorus of roars.

Lemonade sips with a twist of a grin,
"Try to be serious; you can't win!"
Ice cubes clink, sharing secrets so sweet,
Giggling together, they can't be beat.

Coffee beans roast with a whimsical cheer,
Whispering tales that we hold dear.
The teapot's bubbling a funny old tune,
As it spills stories under the moon.

So grab your mug, let the laughter flow,
In every sip, let the good times grow.
Together we'll savor, and let spirits rise,
In the echoes of laughter, where joy never dies!

Tropical Rams and Liquid Dreams

In a land where coconuts boast,
The rams wear shades, sipping the most.
Surfboards dance on a gentle tide,
While llamas in flip-flops glide.

Beneath the palm trees, laughter's found,
A goat in a hammock, spinning 'round.
With tiki drinks and fruit on top,
These party animals just can't stop.

They toast to bananas, juicy and bright,
With parrots that squawk with pure delight.
Each sip's a giggle, each splash a cheer,
In this paradise, there's nothing to fear.

So join the rams, take a dive,
In the comical waves, we all thrive.
With liquid dreams flowing so free,
This is the place we all wish to be.

Golden Sun and Silken Sips

Golden rays kiss the ocean's face,
While turtles waddle with charming grace.
Sipping smoothies, or so it seems,
Diving deep into silken dreams.

Mangoes dance in a dazzling swirl,
As beach balls bounce and seagulls twirl.
Sandy toes in the warmth we bask,
With dolphins joining, a joyous task.

Pineapple hats on crabs so proud,
They throw a party and sing out loud.
In every bubble, laughter shines,
As seahorses sip on twisted lines.

With the sun ablaze, we take our cheer,
Silken sips make worries disappear.
Let's raise our glasses to days so bright,
In this whimsical world, pure delight.

Treats from the Eden of Waves

In a cove where the jellybeans grow,
Waves sprinkle treats with a playful flow.
A clam in a chef's hat stirs delight,
Preparing a feast for the nighttime bite.

Palm trees sway with candy canes,
Dancing crabs play matching games.
With licorice ropes as surfboards glide,
Every taste bud's on a magical ride.

Gummy sharks swim in a fizzy sea,
While frosty mugs hold joy, you'll see.
Each scoop of joy, a sugary gulp,
This Eden of waves makes hearts begin to sulk.

So, grab a treat, don't be shy,
In this wave of flavors, we laugh and sigh.
With wild snacks flying from branches high,
It's a sweet escape, oh my, oh my!

Enchanted Sips of Warmth

On an island where the sun's a friend,
And sips of warmth seem never to end.
A squirrel serving drinks with flair,
In a tiny hat, what a funny affair!

Blenders whirl with a cheerful song,
As pineapples dance and groove along.
Each sip contains a chuckle or two,
In this magical place, where laughter is due.

A turtle winks from his leafy seat,
As flamingos tap to the tropical beat.
Marshmallows float in rum drinks galore,
A paradise party, who could want more?

So raise your glass to this sunny space,
With enchanted sips and a smile on your face.
In this world of laughter and delight,
Every moment shines, oh, what a sight!

Ambrosial Adventures

In a land where fruit flies dance,
Coconut hats wear a funky stance.
Mangoes laugh, they've got the moves,
While guavas claim their groovy grooves.

Pineapple dreams float on a breeze,
Hilarity bursts like puddles of cheese.
Strawberries giggle in twinkling skies,
As fruit-loving pals declare their pies.

Banana boats sail syrupy seas,
Lemons chuckle in the cool, sweet breeze.
Watermelon whispers, 'Grab a slice!'
And to taste it all would be so nice!

With every bite, a joke unfurls,
In this fruity realm where laughter swirls.
So hop aboard this snack parade,
Where silliness blooms in every shade.

Chasing Sunbeams

Beneath the sun where shadows play,
We chase the light in a silly way.
With flip-flops slapping on sandy shores,
Every giggle opens new doors.

Lime green waves roll with a laugh,
As we attempt the hula dance craft.
Silly napping on beach-blanket dreams,
We sip cool drinks topped with whipped cream.

Seagulls squawk like they own the sky,
While we toss chips as they swoop by.
Each sunbeam a tickle, a playful boast,
In this game of fun, we love the most.

When twilight calls for a curtsy bow,
We promise tomorrow our shenanigans vow.
With sunlight's farewell, the laughter remains,
In chasing sunbeams, joy never wanes.

Sip of the Tropics

In a glass, the colors swirl,
Together they dance, a tropical twirl.
Feeling fruity, we toast with flair,
With each sip, a giggle to share.

Coconut giggles, and mango sings,
Banana peels wear the silliest bling.
Every sip brings laughter and cheer,
As flavors burst, we know no fear.

The pink of a guava slips on a smile,
And every rich taste compels us to stay awhile.
With straws like snakes and ice cubes that jive,
In this cup of delight, we feel so alive.

So raise your glass to this merry delight,
In the tropics, each gulp feels just right.
Let's sip on happiness, let nothing be grim,
In our fruity fiesta, let's take a swim!

Melodies in a Mug

In a mug so bright, a tune begins,
Coffee beans tapping, while cinnamon grins.
With every sip, a melody plays,
As friendly froth joins the sing-along ways.

Marshmallows bouncing, a sweet little beat,
As hot cocoa dances on happy feet.
The spoons start swirling, a chorus declared,
In this caffeinated world, we're unprepared.

Jazz notes fizzle with chocolate delight,
While the cupcakes twirl, their frosting takes flight.
Panic not! It's just dessert in disguise,
As laughter bubbles up under sugary skies.

So let the mugs serenade our hearts,
With each cuppa joy, the fun never departs.
In melodies sipped, in laughter we plug,
We'll hum all day long with our joyous mug.

Hidden Harvests in Crystal Glass

In a glass, secrets bloom like flowers,
Grapes giggle, hinting at their powers.
Each sip whispers tales of cheer,
While lemons laugh, they taste a bit queer.

Bubbles dance, how they jest and twirl,
Tickling tongues, a flavor whirl.
Pineapple plots with coconut sly,
Jokes blend in, oh my, oh my!

Peachy keen, the stories unfold,
As cherries tease with hues of gold.
Fruit's comedy, a sweet parade,
In every drop, mischief's laid.

When spills occur, we all join in,
Who needs a glass when we can win?
Slurping joy from nature's stash,
Hidden gems in every splash!

Exotic Embrace of Warm Raindrops

Raindrops patter like giggles above,
In their embrace, we find the love.
Coconut clouds float down so light,
Tasting summer's sheer delight.

Each splash is a dance, a cheerful spree,
A puddle forms a mini sea.
Bananas and mangoes take the lead,
Joking their way with every bead.

Laughter mingles with the storm,
In vibrant drops, every shape and form.
The air gets thick with fruity glee,
Each drench a splash of jubilee.

When umbrellas laugh and hats get wet,
It's the performance we won't forget.
Nature's quirk, so sly and bold,
In warm rain, pure joy unfolds!

Sips Beneath a Canopy of Stars

Under the stars, we share a toast,
To flavors bold, we laugh the most.
Jupiter smiles with a juicy grin,
As comets pass, we sip and spin.

Constellations mix in cups of cheer,
With every gulp, the cosmos near.
Milkshake moons and cherry suns,
Galactic fun, oh what a run!

Underneath this twinkling sea,
Strawberry dreams float wild and free.
Laughter echoes in the midnight air,
Sweet nectar flows; we haven't a care.

Sips of the universe, quirky and bright,
Every flavor in this playful night.
A banquet of stars, all shining clear,
Join the dance, we're all in gear!

Roaming the Oceans in Flavors

A sea of flavors, ride the wave,
Tuna tickles, so bold and brave.
Salty laughter from seaweed's grin,
Dancing octopuses draw us in.

Mussels murmur with tasty tales,
While shrimp wear hats like tiny sails.
Sipping the brine, what a riot,
A sea shanty, oh can we try it?

Fishy jokes, oh what a catch,
In the ocean we'll botch and scratch.
With flavors swirling, tides will tease,
All aboard for a taste of ease!

With every splash, a giggle flows,
Seaweed wiggles where the fun grows.
Join the feast, no need to panic,
Ocean's humor, simply gigantic!

www.ingramcontent.com/pod-product-compliance
Lightning Source LLC
Chambersburg PA
CBHW072221070526
44585CB00015B/1444